BROWN SCHOOL
LIBRARY

DISCARD

A VIEW of the OBELISK erected under LIBERTY-TREE in BOSTON

To every Lover of LIBERTY, this Plate is humbly

LIBERTY BOOK

Leonard Everett Fisher's

LIBERTY BOOK

Doubleday & Company
Garden City, New York
1976

*For My Children
Julie, Susan and James
with love*

Novus Ordo Seclorum

Library of Congress Cataloging in Publication Data
Fisher, Leonard Everett
Leonard Everett Fisher's
Liberty Book

1. United States — History — Revolution, 1775-1783 —
Pictorial works. I. Title.
E209.F52   973.3'022'2
ISBN 0-385-04892-0 Trade
0-385-04894-7 Prebound
Library of Congress Catalog Card Number 75-9672
Copyright © 1976 by Leonard Everett Fisher
All Rights Reserved
Printed in the United States of America
Calligraphy by Joseph Ascherl
9 8 7 6 5 4 3 2

LIBERTY

One cannot stir the ideas of eighteenth-century America without having a ghostly chorus of our antecedents cry out "liberty." Like a musical crescendo, the word *liberty* roars and leaps at us with increasing frequency as events rush toward nationhood. It appears everywhere—on documents and notices; coins, flags and drums; in songs and engravings; slogans and speeches—everywhere. It was there even when not spelled out L-I-B-E-R-T-Y.

With the imposition of the Stamp Tax in 1765, the word *liberty* begins to jab us. By the time the colonists had suffered more repressive measures and the agonies of war, *liberty* overtakes us. It invades our consciousness with the same unyielding force that drove our forbears to court their destruction in defense of their cause.

"I must study politics and war," said John Adams, "that my sons may have the *liberty* to study mathematics and philosophy, geography, natural history, naval architecture, navigation, commerce and agriculture, in order to give their children the right to study painting, music, architecture, statuary, tapestry and porcelain."

This incisive remark should be our legacy today. That it is, as yet, an unfulfilled promise for many, does not destroy, two hundred years later, the reach of John Adams' integrity, humanity and high purpose. That America and Americans still throb with such promise while continuing the battle for *liberty*—for the right of the nation and all of its people to endure in freedom, safety and comfort—for the right of every individual to be heard in government while pursuing his or her own destiny within the structure of this alterable society as envisioned by the Founding Fathers—is still cause for celebration.

The promotion of *liberty* is solely dependent upon the ambition and perseverance of the people. What follows then, is a visual expression of such persistence when *liberty* overcame tyranny and an example was set for the rest of us.

LIBERTY FOREVER

Proclaim LIBERTY
THROUGHOUT THE LAND
AND TO ALL THE INHABITANTS THEREOF

They that can give up essential *liberty*
to obtain a little temporary safety
deserve neither *liberty* nor safety.
Benjamin Franklin

Always for LIBERTY and the PUBLICK GOOD
Motto of the "Virginia Gazette"
Alexander Purdie, Printer

I will oppose this tyranny at the threshold
though the fabric of *liberty* fall,
and I perish in its ruin.
Samuel Adams

The God who gave us life,
gave us *liberty* at the same time.
Thomas Jefferson

It is expected that humanity and tenderness to women and children will distinguish brave Americans, contending for *liberty*, from infamous mercenary ravagers.
George Washington

Ever since I arrived to a state of manhood, I have felt a sincere passion for *liberty*.
Ethan Allen

At Philadelphia, the Heart-and-Hand Fire Company has expelled Mr. Hughes, the stamp man for that colony. The freemen of Talbot County, in Maryland, have erected a gibbet before the door of the courthouse, twenty feet high, and have hanged on it the effigies of a stamp informer in chains, in terrorem, till the Stamp Act shall be repealed; and have resolved, unanimously, to hold in utter contempt and abhorrence every stamp officer, and every favorer of the Stamp Act, and to have no communication with any such person, not even to speak to him, unless to upbraid him with his baseness. So triumphant is the spirit of liberty everywhere...

JOHN ADAMS

To the Memory of the glorious NINETY-TWO: Members of the Hon'bl House of Representatives of the Massachusetts-Bay, who, undaunted by the insolent Menaces of Villains in Power, from a strict Regard to Conscience and the LIBERTIES of their Constituents, on the 30th of June 1768 ~Voted) NOT TO RESCIND

1.

Come join hand in hand brave Americans all,
And rouse your bold hearts at fair Liberty's call;
No tyrannous acts shall stoppeth your just claim,
Or stain with dishonor America's name.

Chorus:

In Freedom we're born and in Freedom we'll live,
Our purses are ready,
Steady, Friends, Steady.
Not as Slaves, but as Freemen our money we'll give.

2.

Our worthy Forefathers—let's give them a cheer,
To Climates unknown did courageously steer;
Thro' Oceans, to deserts, for freedom they came,
And dying bequeath'd us their freedom and Fame.

Chorus:

3.

Their generous bosoms all dangers despis'd,
So highly, so wisely, their Birthrights they priz'd;
We'll keep what they gave, we will piously keep,
Nor frustrate their toils on the land and the deep.

Chorus:

4.

The tree their own hands had to liberty rear'd;
They lived to behold growing strong and rever'd,
With transport they cry'd, "how our wishes we gain
For our children shall gather the fruits of our pain."

Chorus:

5.

Swarms of placemen and pensioners soon will appear
Like locusts deforming the charms of the year;
Suns vainly will rise, Showers vainly descend,
If we are to drudge for what others shall spend.

Chorus:

6.

Then join hand in hand brave Americans all,
By uniting we stand, by dividing we fall;
In so Righteous a cause let us hope to succeed,
For Heaven approves of each generous deed.

Chorus:

7.

All ages shall speak with amaze and applause,
Of the courage we'll show in support of our laws;
To die we can bear, but to serve we disdain,
For shame is to Freedom more dreadful than pain.

Chorus:

8.

This bumper I crown for our Sovereign's health,
And this for Britannia's glory and wealth;
That wealth and that glory immortal may be,
If she is but just —and if we are but Free.

Chorus:

John Dickinson

WILLIAM JACKSON,

an *IMPORTER*; at the *BRAZEN HEAD,*

North Side of the TOWN-HOUSE, *and Opposite the Town-Pump, in Corn-hill,* BOSTON.

It is desired that the SONS and DAUGHTERS of *LIBERTY*, would not buy any one thing of him, for in so doing they will bring Disgrace upon *themselves*, and their *Posterity*, for *ever* and *ever*, AMEN.

TO THE
DELAWARE
PILOTS.

THE Regard we have for your Characters, and our Desire to promote your future Peace and Safety, are the Occasion of this Third Address to you.

In our second Letter we acquainted you, that the Tea Ship was a Three Decker; We are now informed by good Authority, she is not a Three Decker, but an *old black Ship, without a Head, or any Ornaments.*

THE *Captain* is a *short fat* Fellow, and a little *obstinate* withal.----So much the worse for him.----For, so sure as he *rides rusty*, We shall heave him Keel out, and see that his Bottom be well fired, scrubb'd and paid.----His Upper-Works too, will have an Overhawling.----and as it is said, he has a good deal of *Quick Work* about him, We will take particular Care that such Part of him undergoes a thorough Rummaging.

WE have a still *worse* Account of *his Owner*;----for it is said, the Ship POLLY was bought by him on Purpose, to make a Penny of us; and that *he* and Captain *Ayres* were well advised of the Risque they would run, in thus daring to insult and abuse us.

Captain Ayres was here in the Time of the Stamp-Act, and ought to have known our People better, than to have expected we would be so mean as to suffer his *rotten* TEA to be funnel'd down our Throats, with the *Parliament*'s *Duty* mixed with it.

WE know him well, and have calculated to a Gill and a Feather, how much it will require to fit him for an *American Exhibition*. And we hope, not one of your Body will behave so ill, as to oblige us to clap him in the Cart along Side of the *Captain*.

WE must repeat, that the SHIP POLLY is an *old black Ship*, of about Two Hundred and Fifty Tons burthen, *without a Head*, and *without Ornaments*,----and, that CAPTAIN AYRES is a *thick chunky Fellow*.----------As such, TAKE CARE to AVOID THEM.

YOUR OLD FRIENDS,

THE COMMITTEE FOR TARRING AND FEATHERING.

Philadelphia, December 7, 1773.

That the Inhabitants of the English Colonies in North America, by the immutable Laws of Nature, the principles of the English Constitution, and the several charters or compacts, have the following Rights:

Resolved:
That they are entitled to Life, Liberty, and Property, and they have never ceded to any sovereign Power whatever, a Right to dispose of either without their consent.
That our ancestors, who first settled these Colonies, were at the time of their emigration from the mother country, entitled to all the Rights, Liberties, and Immunities of free and natural-born subjects within the Realm of England.

. . .

That the foundation of English Liberty, and of all free government, is a Right in the people to participate in their legislative council . . .

AND **UNION**

LIBERTY TREE

I.

In a chariot of light from the regions of day,
    The Goddess of Liberty came;
Ten thousand celestials directed the way,
    And hither conducted the dame.
A fair budding branch from the gardens above,
    Where millions with millions agree,
She brought in her hand, as a pledge of her love,
    And the plant she named, *Liberty tree*.

II.

The celestial exotic struck deep in the ground,
    Like a native it flourish'd and bore.
The fame of its fruit drew the nations around,
    To seek out this peaceable shore.
Unmindful of names or distinctions they came,
    For freemen like brothers agree,
With one spirit endued, they one friendship pursued,
    And their temple was *Liberty tree*.

III.

Beneath this fair tree, like the patriarchs of old,
    Their bread in contentment they eat,
Unvex'd with the troubles of silver and gold,
    The cares of the grand and the great.
With timber and tar they Old England supply'd,
    And supported her power on the sea;
Her battles they fought, without getting a groat,
    For the honour of *Liberty tree*.

IV.

But hear, O ye swains, ('tis a tale most profane),
    How all the tyrannical powers,
King, Commons, and Lords, are uniting amain,
    To cut down this guardian of ours;
From the east to the west, blow the trumpet to arms,
    Thro' the land let the sound of it flee,
Let the far and the near,—all unite with a cheer,
    In defence of our *Liberty tree*.

Thomas Paine

Three millions of people, armed in the holy cause of *liberty*, and in such a country as we possess, are invincible by any force which our enemy can send against us. Besides, sir, we shall not fight our battle alone. There is a just God who presides over the destinies of nations, and who will raise up friends to fight our battles for us. The battle, sir, is not to the strong alone; it is for the vigilant, the active, the brave. Besides, sir, we have no election. If we were base enough to desire it, it is now too late to retire from the contest. There is no retreat but in submission and slavery! Our chains are forged! Their clanking may be heard on the plains of Boston! The war is inevitable—and let it come! I repeat, sir, let it come!

It is in vain, sir, to extenuate the matter. Gentlemen may cry, Peace, Peace — but there is no peace. The war is actually begun! The next gale that sweeps from the north will bring to our ears the clash of resounding arms! Our brethren are already in the field! Why stand we here idle? What is it that gentlemen wish? What would they have? Is life so dear, or peace so sweet, as to be purchased at the price of chains and slavery? Forbid it, Almighty God! I know not what course others may take; but as for me, give me *liberty* or give me death!

Patrick Henry

I FALL FOR LIBERTY

Warren was his country's choice
Called to arms by its voice
Quit drug and pill his post to fill
And take command at Bunker Hill
To repel the tyrant's forces

And then a cursed unlucky shot
Struck Warren in a vital spot
"I fall," cried he, "for Liberty
And gladly bleed if we succeed
Oh, may my country soon be freed!"
Thus died the heroic Warren

Anonymous

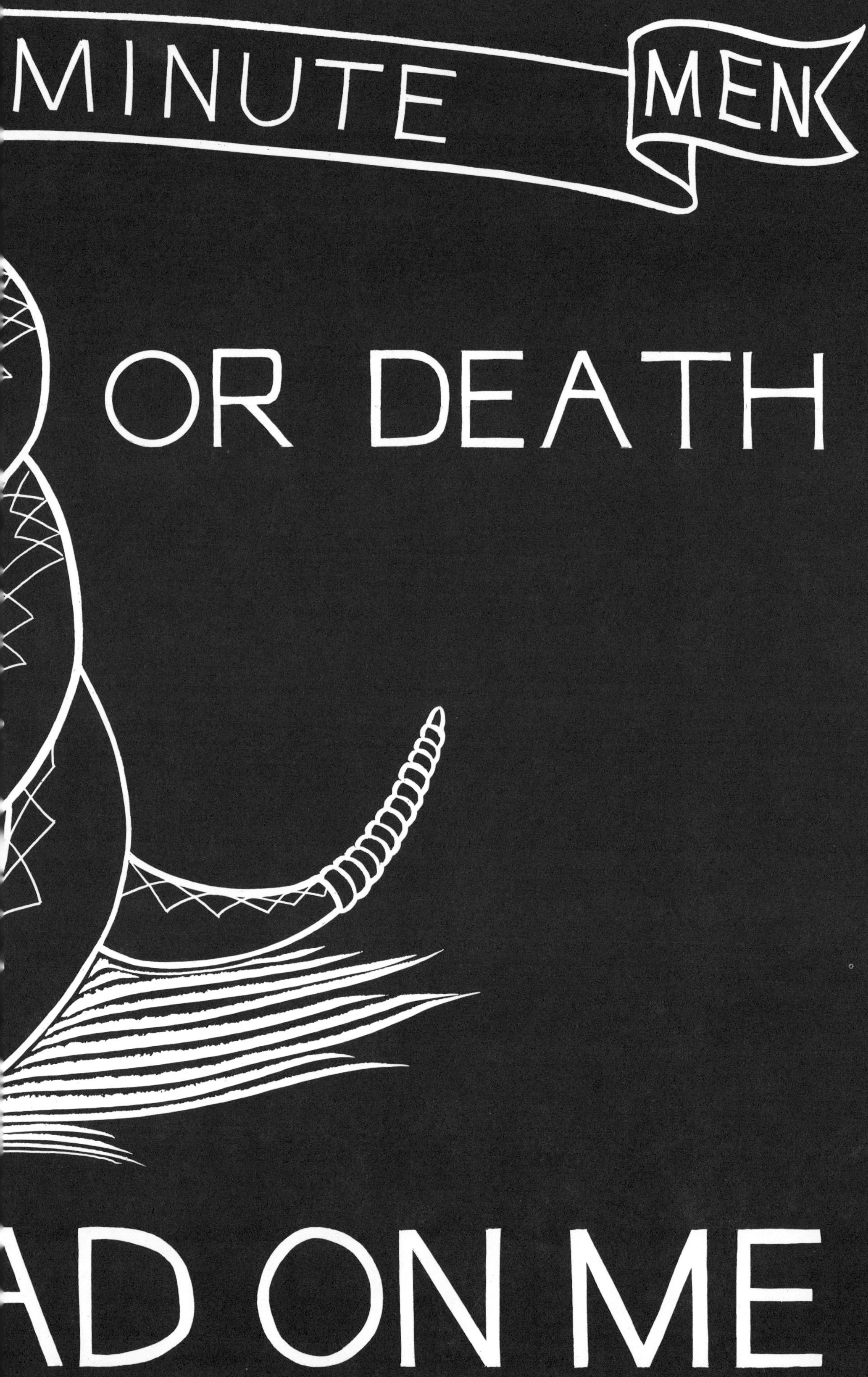
MINUTE MEN
OR DEATH
AD ON ME

The Massachusetts Spy

Or, Thomas's Boston Journal.

'Do thou Great LIBERTY inspire our Souls—And make our Lives in thy Possession happy—Or, our Deaths glorious in thy just Defence.'

JOIN OR DIE

(Vol. V.) THURSDAY, March 9, 1775. (Numb. 214.)

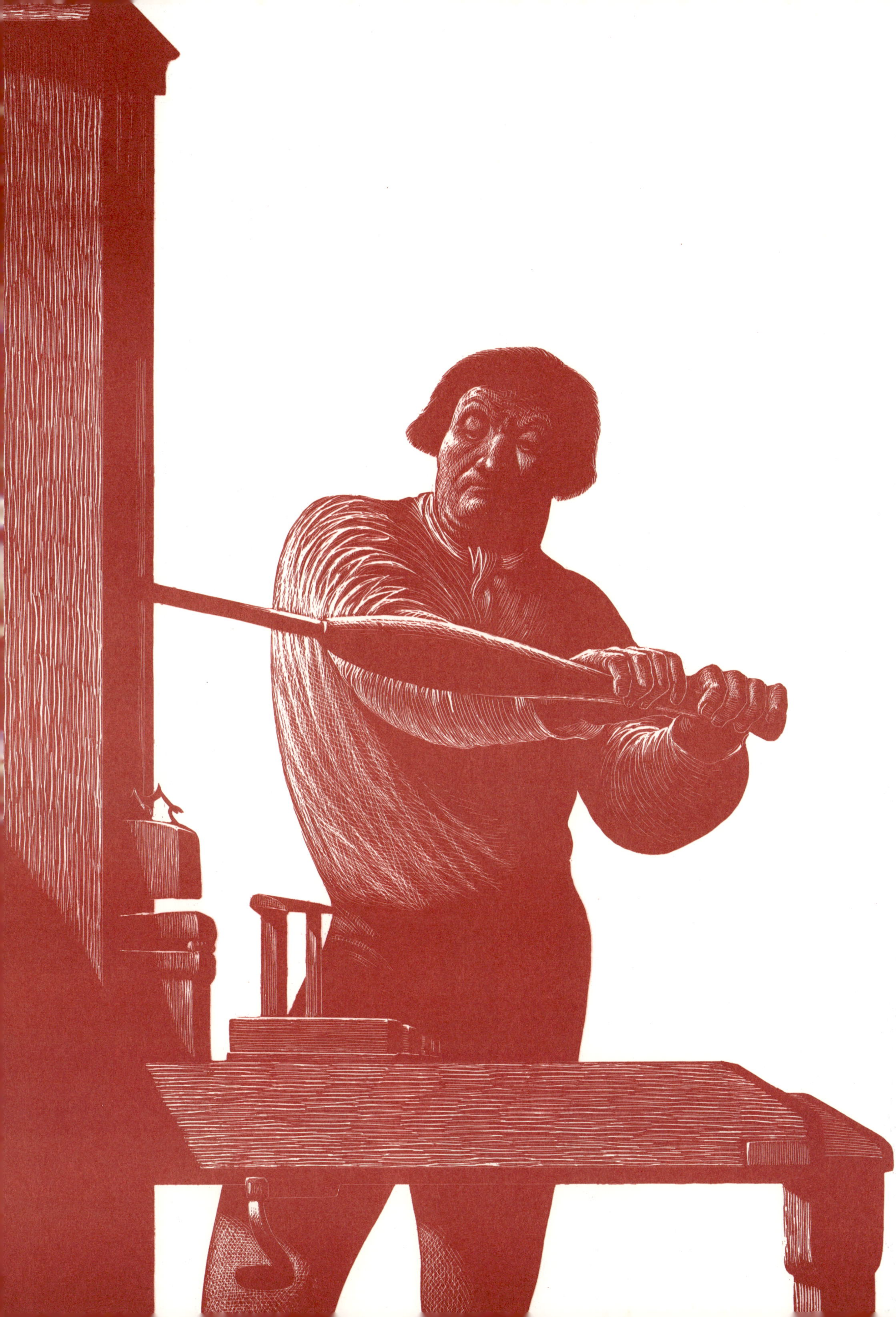

LIBE

RTY

In CONGRESS, July 4, 1776.

A DECLARATION

By the Representatives of the

UNITED STATES OF AMERICA,

In General Congress assembled.

WHEN in the Course of human Events, it becomes necessary for one People to dissolve the Political Bands which have connected them with another, and to assume among the Powers of the Earth, the separate and equal Station to which the Laws of Nature and of Nature's God entitle them, a decent Respect to the Opinions of Mankind requires that they should declare the causes which impel them to the Separation.

We hold these Truths to be self-evident, that all Men are created equal, that they are endowed by their Creator with certain unalienable Rights, that among these are Life, Liberty, and the Pursuit of Happiness—That to secure these Rights, Governments are instituted among Men, deriving their just Powers from the Consent of the Governed, that whenever any Form of Government becomes destructive of these Ends, it is the Right of the People to alter or to abolish it, and to institute new Government, laying its Foundation on such Principles, and organizing its Powers in such Form, as to them shall seem most likely to effect their Safety and Happiness. Prudence, indeed, will dictate that Governments long established should not be changed for light and transient Causes; and accordingly all Experience hath shewn, that Mankind are more disposed to suffer, while Evils are sufferable, than to right themselves by abolishing the Forms to which they are accustomed. But when a long Train of Abuses and Usurpations, pursuing invariably the same Object, evinces a Design to reduce them under absolute Despotism, it is their Right, it is their Duty, to throw off such Government, and to provide new Guards for their future Security. Such has been the patient Sufferance of these Colonies; and such is now the Necessity which constrains them to alter their former Systems of Government. The History of the present King of Great-Britain is a History of repeated Injuries and Usurpations, all having in direct Object the Establishment of an absolute Tyranny over these States. To prove this, let Facts be submitted to a candid World.

He has refused his Assent to Laws, the most wholesome and necessary for the public Good.

He has forbidden his Governors to pass Laws of immediate and pressing Importance, unless suspended in their Operation till his Assent should be obtained; and when so suspended, he has utterly neglected to attend to them.

He has refused to pass other Laws for the Accommodation of large Districts of People, unless those People would relinquish the Right of Representation in the Legislature, a Right inestimable to them, and formidable to Tyrants only.

He has called together Legislative Bodies at Places unusual, uncomfortable, and distant from the Depository of their public Records, for the sole Purpose of fatiguing them into Compliance with his Measures.

He has dissolved Representative Houses repeatedly, for opposing with manly Firmness his Invasions on the Rights of the People.

He has refused for a long Time, after such Dissolutions, to cause others to be elected; whereby the Legislative Powers, incapable of Annihilation, have returned to the People at large for their exercise; the State remaining in the mean time exposed to all the Dangers of Invasion from without, and Convulsions within.

He has endeavoured to prevent the Population of these States; for that Purpose obstructing the Laws for Naturalization of Foreigners; refusing to pass others to encourage their Migrations hither, and raising the Conditions of new Appropriations of Lands.

He has obstructed the Administration of Justice, by refusing his Assent to Laws for establishing Judiciary Powers.

He has made Judges dependent on his Will alone, for the Tenure of their Offices, and the Amount and Payment of their Salaries.

He has erected a Multitude of new Offices, and sent hither Swarms of Officers to harrass our People, and eat out their Substance.

He has kept among us, in Times of Peace, Standing Armies, without the consent of our Legislatures.

He has affected to render the Military independent of and superior to the Civil Power.

He has combined with others to subject us to a Jurisdiction foreign to our Constitution, and unacknowledged by our Laws; giving his Assent to their Acts of pretended Legislation:

For quartering large Bodies of Armed Troops among us:

For protecting them, by a mock Trial, from Punishment for any Murders which they should commit on the Inhabitants of these States:

For cutting off our Trade with all Parts of the World:

For imposing Taxes on us without our Consent:

For depriving us, in many Cases, of the Benefits of Trial by Jury:

For transporting us beyond Seas to be tried for pretended Offences:

For abolishing the free System of English Laws in a neighbouring Province, establishing therein an arbitrary Government, and enlarging its Boundaries, so as to render it at once an Example and fit Instrument for introducing the same absolute Rule into these Colonies:

For taking away our Charters, abolishing our most valuable Laws, and altering fundamentally the Forms of our Governments:

For suspending our own Legislatures, and declaring themselves invested with Power to legislate for us in all Cases whatsoever.

He has abdicated Government here, by declaring us out of his Protection and waging War against us.

He has plundered our Seas, ravaged our Coasts, burnt our Towns, and destroyed the Lives of our People.

He is, at this Time, transporting large Armies of foreign Mercenaries to compleat the Works of Death, Desolation, and Tyranny, already begun with circumstances of Cruelty and Perfidy, scarcely paralleled in the most barbarous Ages, and totally unworthy the Head of a civilized Nation.

He has constrained our fellow Citizens taken Captive on the high Seas to bear Arms against their Country, to become the Executioners of their Friends and Brethren, or to fall themselves by their Hands.

He has excited domestic Insurrections amongst us, and has endeavoured to bring on the Inhabitants of our Frontiers, the merciless Indian Savages, whose known Rule of Warfare, is an undistinguished Destruction, of all Ages, Sexes and Conditions.

In every stage of these Oppressions we have Petitioned for Redress in the most humble Terms: Our repeated Petitions have been answered only by repeated Injury. A Prince, whose Character is thus marked by every act which may define a Tyrant, is unfit to be the Ruler of a free People.

Nor have we been wanting in Attentions to our British Brethren. We have warned them from Time to Time of Attempts by their Legislature to extend an unwarrantable Jurisdiction over us. We have reminded them of the Circumstances of our Emigration and Settlement here. We have appealed to their native Justice and Magnanimity, and we have conjured them by the Ties of our common Kindred to disavow these Usurpations, which, would inevitably interrupt our Connections and Correspondence. They too have been deaf to the Voice of Justice and of Consanguinity. We must, therefore, acquiesce in the Necessity, which denounces our Separation, and hold them, as we hold the rest of Mankind, Enemies in War, in Peace, Friends.

We, therefore, the Representatives of the UNITED STATES OF AMERICA, in GENERAL CONGRESS, Assembled, appealing to the Supreme Judge of the World for the Rectitude of our Intentions, do, in the Name, and by Authority of the good People of these Colonies, solemnly Publish and Declare, That these United Colonies are, and of Right ought to be, FREE AND INDEPENDENT STATES; that they are absolved from all Allegiance to the British Crown, and that all political Connection between them and the State of Great-Britain, is and ought to be totally dissolved; and that as FREE AND INDEPENDENT STATES, they have full Power to levy War, conclude Peace, contract Alliances, establish Commerce, and to do all other Acts and Things which INDEPENDENT STATES may of right do. And for the support of this Declaration, with a firm Reliance on the Protection of divine Providence, we mutually pledge to each other our Lives, our Fortunes, and our sacred Honor.

Signed by Order and in Behalf of the Congress,

JOHN HANCOCK, President.

ATTEST.
CHARLES THOMSON, Secretary.

Philadelphia: Printed by John Dunlap.

We hold these Truths to be self-evident,
that all Men are created equal,
that they are endowed by their Creator
with certain unalienable Rights,
that among these are
Life,
Liberty
and the
Pursuit of Happiness.
That to secure these Rights,
Governments are instituted among Men,
deriving their just Powers from the
Consent of the Governed . . .

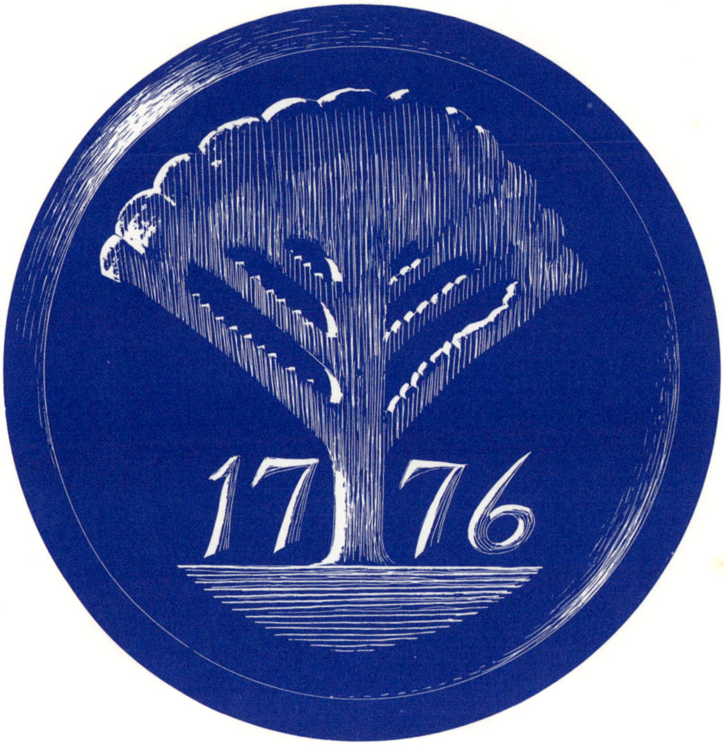
1776

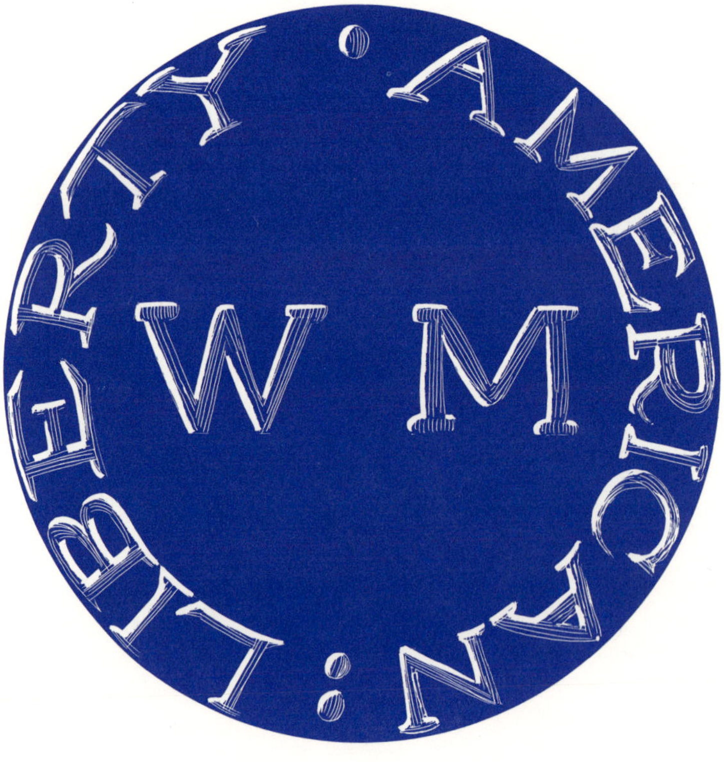
AMERICAN : LIBERTY
W M

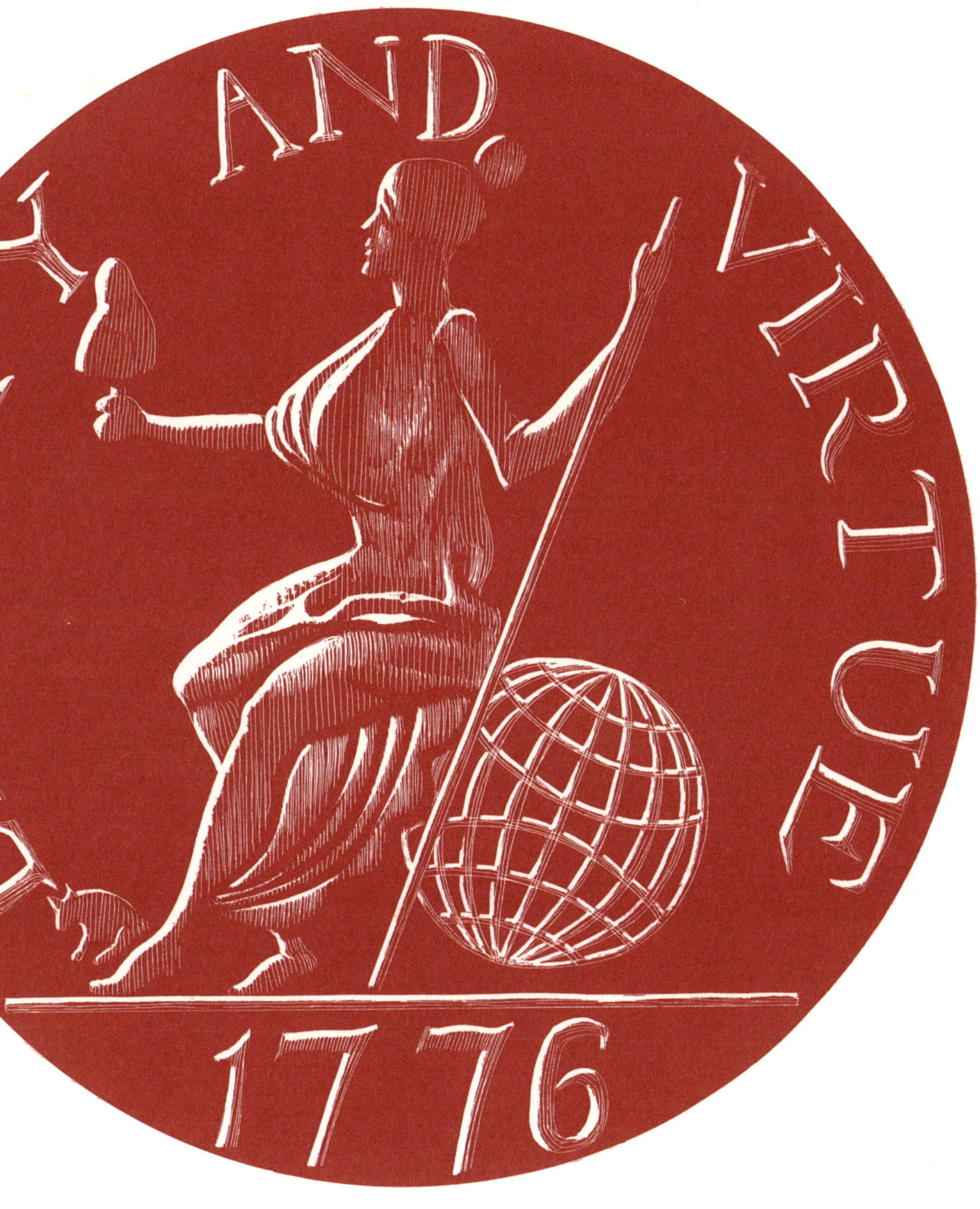
LIBERTY AND VIRTUE
1776

Whereas *the Delegates of the United States of America in Congress assembled did on the fifteenth day of November in the Year of Our Lord One Thousand Seven Hundred and Seventy-Seven, and in the Second Year of the Independence of America agree to certain articles of Confederation and perpetual Union between the States of Newhampshire, Massachusettes-bay, Rhodeisland and Providence Plantations, Connecticut, New York, New Jersey, Pennsylvania, Delaware, Maryland, Virginia, North-Carolina, South-Carolina, and Georgia in the words following, viz.*

Article I. *The stile of this confederacy shall be "The United States of America."*

Article II. *Each State retains its sovereignty, freedom and independence, and every power, jurisdiction and right, which is not by this confederation expressly delegated to the United States, in Congress assembled.*

Article III. *The said States hereby severally enter into a firm league of friendship with each other, for their common defence, the security of their liberties, and their mutual and general welfare, binding themselves to assist each other, against all force offered to, or attacks made upon them, or any of them, on account of religion, sovereignty, trade, or any other pretence whatever.*

We the People
of the United States,
in order to form
a more perfect Union,
establish Justice,
insure domestic Tranquility,
provide for the common defence,
promote the general Welfare,
and
secure the Blessings of *Liberty*
to ourselves and our Posterity,
do ordain and establish
this Constitution
for the
United States of America.

Hail, Columbia

Hail Co-lum-bia, hap-py land, Hail, ye he-roes, Heav'n born band, Who fought and bled in Free-dom's cause, Who fought and bled in Free-dom's cause, And when the storm of war was gone, En-joyed the peace your val-or won, Let

Im-mor-tal pa-triots rise once more De-fend your rights, de-fend your shores, Let no rude foe with im-pi-ous hand, Let no rude foe with im-pi-ous hand, In-vade the shrine where sa-cred lies, Of toil and blood the well-earn'd prize, While

Sound, sound the trump of fame, Let Wash-ing-ton's great name, Let Ring thro' the world with loud ap-plause, Ring thro' the world with loud ap-plause, Let ev-'ry clime to free-dom dear, Lis-ten with a joy-ful ear, With

HAIL, COLUMBIA. Arranged by Robert S. Keller. From SONGS FOR CHILDREN, Everybody's Favorite Series #5. © Copyright MCMXXXIV Amsco Music Publishing Company, Division of Music Sales Corporation, New York. Used by permission.

in - de - pend - ence be our boast, Ev - er mind - ful what it cost,
off - 'ring peace sin - cere and just In Heav'n we place a man - ly trust, That
e - qual skill with God - like pow'r, He gov - erns in the fear - ful hour, Of

Ev - er grate - ful for the prize, Let it's al - tar reach the skies.
truth and jus - tice will pre - vail, And ev - 'ry scheme of bond - age fail.
hor - rid war or guides with ease, The hap - pier times of hon - est peace.

Firm, u - ni - ted let us be, Ral - ly - ing 'round our lib - er - ty;

As a band of broth - ers joined, Peace and safe - ty we shall find.

THE NEW COLOSSUS

Not like the brazen giant of Greek fame,
    With conquering limbs astride from land to land;
    Here at our sea-washed, sunset gates shall stand
A mighty woman with a torch, whose flame
Is the imprisoned lightning, and her name
    Mother of Exiles. From her beacon-hand
    Glows world-wide welcome; her mild eyes command
The air-bridges harbor that twin cities frame.
"Keep ancient lands, your storied pomp!" cries she
    With silent lips. "Give me your tired, your poor,
Your huddled masses yearning to breathe free,
    The wretched refuse of your teeming shore.
Send these, the homeless, tempest-tost to me,
    I lift my lamp beside the golden door!"

Emma Lazarus

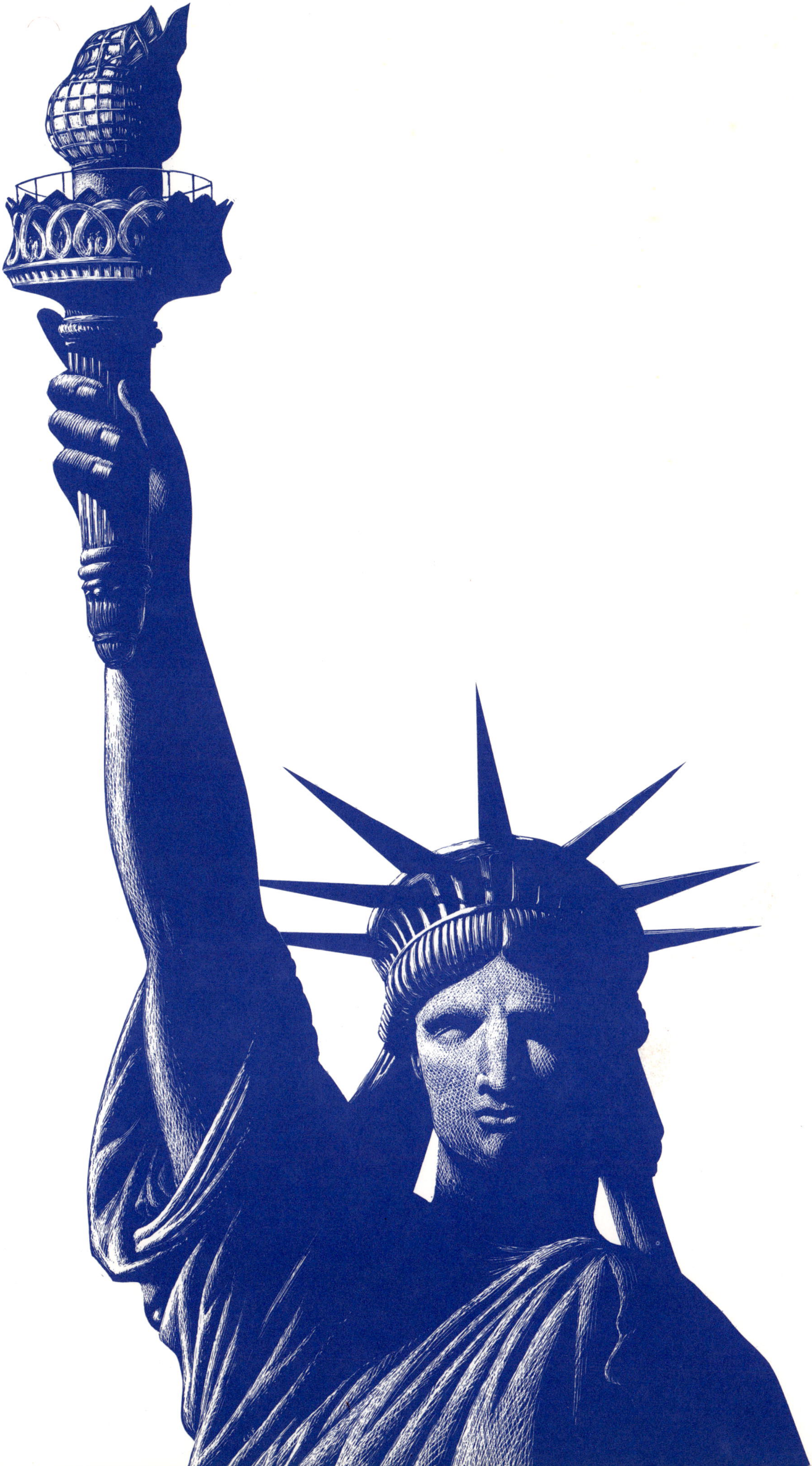

NOTES ON THE MATERIAL

Endpapers: "The Obelisk" was engraved by Paul Revere in 1766 to commemorate the repeal of the Stamp Act.
Courtesy, American Antiquarian Society

Pages 6-7: The Liberty Bell was first cast in London in 1752 to celebrate the fiftieth anniversary of the Commonwealth of Pennsylvania. It cracked while being tested and was recast in Philadelphia in 1753. It cracked again in 1835 while tolling the death of John Marshall, Chief Justice of the United States. The text "Proclaim Liberty . . ." appears on the bell and is biblical in origin (Leviticus 25:10).

Page 10: From the diary of John Adams, January 2, 1766.

Page 12: The dedication engraved on the "Liberty Bowl"—a silver bowl created by Paul Revere in 1768 upon a commission of the Sons of Liberty. The bowl honored the Massachusetts legislators who refused to withdraw an anti-British resolution. The piece is in the collection of the Boston Museum of Fine Arts.

Pages 14-15: The "Liberty Song" first appeared in the Boston *Gazette*, July 1768. John Dickinson, the author, wrote the words to fit an old tune—"Hearts of Oak."
Courtesy, The Historical Society of Pennsylvania

Pages 16-17: *Liberty* was a sloop owned by John Hancock. In June 1768, she was seized by the British when Hancock refused to pay duty on a cargo of wine he had brought to his Boston dock. Hancock had the customs officers seized, thrown overboard and otherwise manhandled by a mob of the Sons of Liberty.

Page 18: A boycott broadside, c.1770.
Courtesy, Massachusetts Historical Society

Page 20: A tea importation broadside, December 1773.
Courtesy, The Historical Society of Pennsylvania; from the Collections of the Library Company of Philadelphia

Page 21: An extract from the Declarations and Resolves, First Continental Congress, October 14, 1774.

Pages 22-23: The flag of the Taunton, Massachusetts, "Separationists," 1774.

Pages 24-25: The Liberty Tree stood near the Boston Common. Here, patriots protested while Tories were hanged in effigy or tarred and feathered. The British cut the tree down. The poem was written in 1775.

Pages 26-27: An excerpt from Patrick Henry's remarks at the Virginia Provincial Assembly, March 23, 1775.

Pages 28-29: Dr. Joseph Warren, a much respected physician, was one of Boston's chief radical leaders.

Pages 30-31: The flag of the Culpeper, Virginia, Minutemen, 1775.

Page 33: The masthead of *The Massachusetts Spy*, a patriot Boston newspaper published by Isaiah Thomas.
Courtesy, Massachusetts Historical Society

Pages 34-35: The flag of Colonel William Moultrie. It was flown during the defense of Fort Sullivan, Charleston, South Carolina, June 28, 1776.

Page 36: The first official printed text of the Declaration of Independence, 1776.
Courtesy, The Pequot Library, Southport, Connecticut

Page 38: Pure copper coin patterns authorized by New Hampshire in 1776. The initials "W.M." indicate the mint master, William Moulton.

Page 39: The reverse side of a Pine Tree Copper cent issued in 1776 by Massachusetts.

Page 40: An extract from The Articles of Confederation, Second Continental Congress. Ratified March 1, 1781.

Page 41: The Preamble to the Constitution. Ratified June 21, 1788.

Pages 42-43: "Hail, Columbia" was a wordless patriotic hymn composed by Philip Phile in 1789. It was known as "The President's March" until 1798 when Joseph Hopkinson added the words.

Pages 44-45: The Statue of Liberty in New York Harbor was a French gift to the United States. It was given to commemorate Franco-American friendship; the American and French Revolutions; and the first hundred years of American independence. The statue was the work of French sculptor Frederic Auguste Bertholdi. It was dedicated by President Grover Cleveland, October 28, 1886. A bronze tablet bearing the poem *The New Colossus*, written in 1883, was fixed to the base of the statue in 1903.

Leonard Everett Fisher, painter, illustrator, author, and educator, was born and raised in New York City. His formal art training began at the Heckscher Foundation in 1932 and was completed at the Yale School of Art and Architecture after his wartime military service. At Yale, he received Bachelor and Master degrees in Fine Arts and the Winchester Fellowship. In 1950, Mr. Fisher received a Pulitzer painting prize. The following year he was named dean of the Whitney School of Art in New Haven, Connecticut. He resigned from that post in 1953 and turned his attention to children's literature. Since then he has illustrated some two hundred books — chiefly for children — about thirty of which he has written, including *The Death of Evening Star, The Warlock of Westfall and Sweeney's Ghost*. In addition, Mr. Fisher has designed six United States postage stamps, five of which commemorate the Bicentennial Era. More recently he created thirteen posters dealing with the American Revolution. He has been cited by The American Institute of Graphic Arts, The Connecticut League of Historical Societies and The New York *Times*, among others. In 1968, the Fifth International Book Fair, Bologna, Italy, awarded him its Premio Grafico for juvenile illustration. Mr. Fisher's art is represented in such diverse collections as The Butler Art Institute, Ohio; Mount Holyoke College Art Museum, Massachusetts; The Library of Congress, Washington, D.C.; The New Britain Museum of American Art, Connecticut; The Free Library of Philadelphia, Pennsylvania; and the Universities of Oregon, Minnesota and Southern Mississippi. In 1973, The New Britain Museum honored him with a twenty-four-year retrospective exhibition. Currently a faculty member of The Paier School of Art in Hamden, Connecticut, Mr. Fisher makes his home with his wife Margery and their three children in Westport, Connecticut.

A VIEW of the OBELISK erected under LIBERTY-TREE in BOSTON

To every Lover of LIBERTY, this Plate is humbly

BROWN SCHOOL
LIBRARY

DATE DUE			
FEB 1			
MAY 1			
MAR.			
NOV. 1 3 1987			
OCT. 0 3 1988			
12			
13			